Fact Finders™

Biographies

Benjamin Banneker

Astronomer and Mathematician

by Allison Lassieur

Consultant:
Steven X. Lee, Director
Benjamin Banneker Historical Park and Museum
Baltimore, Maryland

Capstone *press*

Mankato, Minnesota

Fact Finders is published by Capstone Press,
151 Good Counsel Drive, P.O. Box 669, Mankato, Minnesota 56002.
www.capstonepress.com

Library of Congress Cataloging-in-Publication Data
Lassieur, Allison.
    Benjamin Banneker : astronomer and mathematician / by Allison Lassieur.
    p. cm. — (Fact finders. Biographies)
    Includes bibliographical references and index.
    ISBN-13: 978-0-7368-5432-0 (hardcover)
    ISBN-10: 0-7368-5432-0 (hardcover)
    1. Banneker, Benjamin, 1731–1806. 2. Astronomers—United States—Biography—Juvenile
literature. 3. Scientists—United States—Biography—Juvenile literature. 4. Mathematicians—
United States—Biography—Juvenile literature. 5. African American scientists—Biography—
Juvenile literature. 6. African American mathematicians—Biography—Juvenile literature. I. Title.
II. Series.
QB36.B22L368 2006
520'.92—dc22   2005022577

Summary: An introduction to the life of Benjamin Banneker, the African American astronomer
    and mathematician who helped survey Washington, D.C., and who wrote several
    successful almanacs.

Editorial Credits
Megan Schoeneberger, editor; Juliette Peters, set designer and illustrator; Linda Clavel and
    Scott Thoms, book designers; Kelly Garvin, photo researcher/photo editor

Photo Credits
Archives Center, National Museum of American History, Behring Center, Smithsonian Institution,
11; Courtesy of the Massachusetts Historical Society, 23; Getty Images Inc./Hulton Archive,
22; The Granger Collection, New York, 1, 9, 21, 25, 26; Library of Congress, 4–5, 14–15, 16; The
Maryland Historical Society, Baltimore, Maryland, 17; North Wind/North Wind Picture Archives,
12; Photographs and Prints Division, The Schomberg Center for Research in Black Culture, The
New York Public Library, Astor, Lenox and Tilden Foundation, cover, 18–19, 27

1 2 3 4 5 6 11 10 09 08 07 06

Table of Contents

Chapter 1

Planning a City

In 1791, a gray-haired man stood on a hilltop. A wilderness spread out below him. Soon, a great city would be built on the land. The city, Washington, D.C., would be the capital of the United States.

The man, Benjamin Banneker, was there to help plan the city. He was the only black member of a small team. Their job was to **survey** the land. Together, they would figure out where buildings in the new city would be built. Banneker got the job because of his math and **astronomy** skills.

The city of Washington, D.C., was built along the Potomac River.

Banneker was a free black man at a time when most blacks were slaves. His work with the surveying team made him one of the most respected scientists of the 1700s.

Chapter 2

Growing Up

Benjamin Banneker was born November 9, 1731, near Baltimore, Maryland. Banneker's parents, Mary and Robert, were free. So were Banneker's grandparents.

Banneker's grandmother was white. She had come to America from England in 1683. She owned a small farm and two slaves. In time, she freed her slaves and married one of them. Their daughter was Banneker's mother.

When Banneker was 6 years old, his father bought a farm. He grew tobacco and corn. Banneker helped care for the animals and harvest the crops. His father taught him to study the sky for signs of rain or stormy weather.

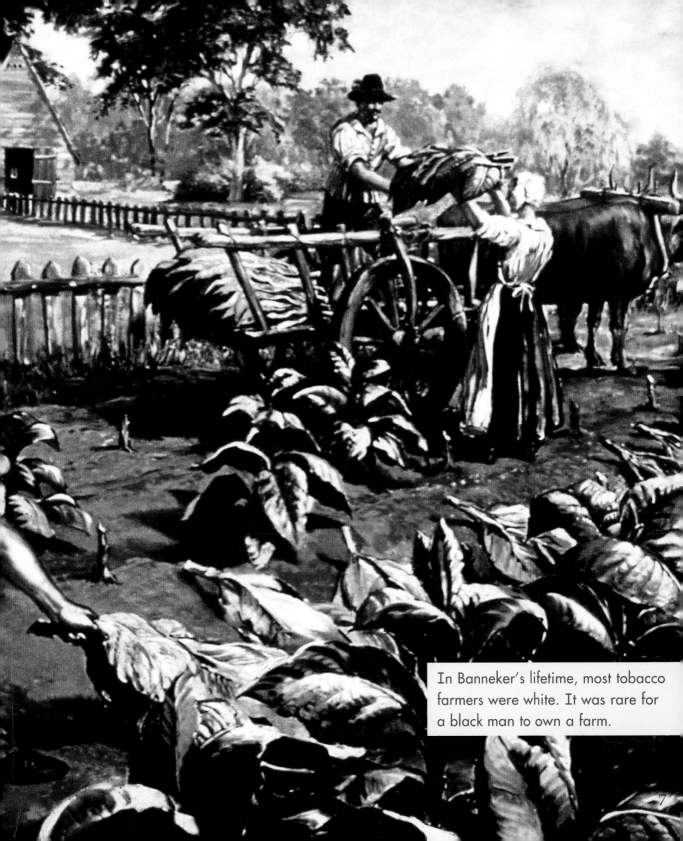

In Banneker's lifetime, most tobacco farmers were white. It was rare for a black man to own a farm.

Banneker's grandmother took a special interest in her grandson. She taught him to read and write. She used her Bible as the lesson book.

School

During winter, Banneker went to a school run by a religious group called the **Quakers**. It was unusual for a black child to go to school at that time. But the Quakers believed all people should be treated equally. Banneker loved reading and math.

In the 1700s, most schools accepted only white students. Banneker was lucky to go to school, even if it was for a short time.

After a few years, Banneker was old enough to help his father on the farm full time. He quit school but continued to teach himself. Banneker borrowed books when he could. He studied math on his own.

Chapter 3

A Wooden Clock

When Banneker was about 22 years old, he met a man who had a pocket watch. Banneker was fascinated by the watch. He asked to borrow it.

Banneker studied the watch. He took it apart piece by piece to see how it worked. He drew pictures of the wheels and gears inside. Then he decided to build one of his own.

The only material Banneker had to work with was wood. He couldn't possibly carve wood into such tiny parts for a watch. So he decided to carve bigger pieces and build a clock.

Banneker's wooden clock probably looked like this one.

Banneker collected
pieces of wood and
carefully carved them. He
bought springs, the chime,
and a few other pieces
that could not be made of
wood. After many months,
the clock was finished.

American Clock

Banneker's clock
was the first made with
parts entirely from North
America. Other people had
built clocks, but they had
used European parts.

Banneker was a
quiet, serious man. ⬇

Banneker's clock made him famous. People were amazed that a black man had the talent to build such a clock. At that time, many people thought that black people were not as smart as white people.

People traveled from distant towns to see Banneker's clock. Banneker was happy to show it to anyone who asked. People who had never heard of this quiet farmer now knew all about Banneker and his wooden clock.

QUOTE

"With his inferior tools, with no other model than a borrowed watch, it had cost him long and patient labor to perfect it."
—a relative of Banneker's friend, describing Banneker's clock

Chapter 4

Looking to the Sky

By the time Banneker was 30 years old, both his grandmother and his father had died. Banneker farmed his father's land and sold crops. In his spare time, he read books. He also taught himself to play the flute and the violin. At the end of a hard day, Banneker enjoyed playing music.

Word of Banneker's reading and math abilities spread throughout the area. At the time, few people, black or white, could read. Many of Banneker's white neighbors asked him to read letters they received. They also asked him to repair their broken clocks.

Banneker's farm was near
Ellicott Mills, Maryland.

Banneker was happy to help them.
He treated them with respect and
kindness. Slowly, he gained their respect
in return. Banneker became well-known
and admired in his community.

Early astronomers used
telescopes and compasses
to study the night sky. ▼

Banneker became close friends with his neighbor George Ellicott. Their friendship grew over many years.

The Night Sky

Sometime in the late 1780s, Ellicott gave Banneker three astronomy books. He also gave Banneker some simple instruments for studying the sky.

Banneker had learned how to read the sky from his father, but he had never studied the science of astronomy. He read the books and taught himself how to use the instruments.

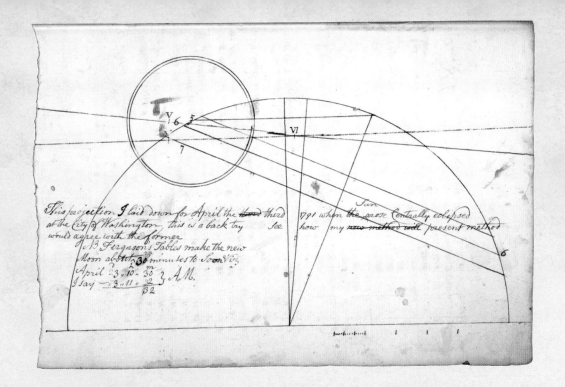

This projection I laid down for April the ~~third~~ third 1791 when the ~~arose~~ arose Centrally eclipsed at the City of Washington, this is a back try. See how my ~~new method will~~ present method would agree with the former
N.B Ferguson's Tables make the new Moon about 30 minutes to Soon Viz.
April 3.10..30 ⅔ A.M.
I say 3..11.. 2/32 ⅔ A.M.

▲ In his journal, Banneker made careful records of what he saw in the sky.

Banneker loved studying the stars. He spent his nights looking at the sky and his days sleeping. His mind was on fire with new ideas about astronomy. Banneker had found a new direction for his life as a scientist of the stars.

FACT!

Banneker successfully predicted a solar eclipse in 1791.

Chapter 5

New Adventures

In early 1791, Banneker was 59 years old. That year, the U.S. government hired George Ellicott's brother, Andrew, to help survey land for a new capital city. Andrew needed a scientist to be on his surveying team. He remembered Banneker's skills with astronomy and math. Andrew asked Banneker to join the team. He agreed.

In February, the team arrived at the Potomac River to begin planning the new city. Banneker helped make **observations** and record information.

Banneker was the only black man on the team that surveyed the land for Washington, D.C.

"I procured [hired] him [Benjamin Banneker] to be employed under one of our chief directors in laying out the new federal city . . . he is a very worthy and respectable member of society."

—Thomas Jefferson

Banneker and his coworkers used compasses, telescopes, and clocks to measure distances. Then, other team members tramped through the forest with surveying chains. They marked the placement of each street and building in the new city. Later, workers chopped down trees to clear the land.

A few months later, Banneker's part of the job was finished. He packed up his belongings and returned to his farm.

Almanacs

Banneker returned to his study of astronomy. Soon he decided to publish an **almanac**. Almanacs are books filled with weather **predictions**, advice for farmers, short stories, and sometimes poetry. Banneker used astronomy and math to make the predictions for his almanac.

Banneker's almanac created a sensation. Most people thought that blacks couldn't understand things like science and math. Banneker's almanac proved that black people are just as smart as everyone else.

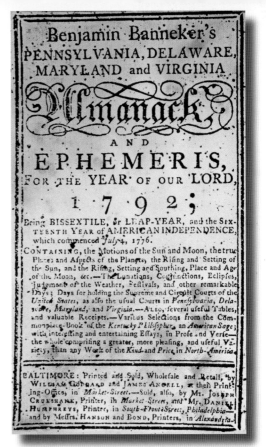

▲ Banneker published his first almanac in 1792.

QUOTE

"I consider this Negro as fresh proof that the powers of the mind are disconnected with the color of the skin."
—James McHenry, in the introduction to the 1792 edition of Banneker's almanac

A Bold Letter

In August 1791, Banneker sent a letter to U.S. Secretary of State Thomas Jefferson. He also included a copy of his almanac. In the letter, Banneker explained that he believed that slavery was wrong. He also said that he was proof that black people were intelligent and creative. It was a bold letter for a black man to write.

Jefferson sent Banneker a kind response. He promised to send the almanac to the Royal Academy of Sciences in Paris, France, as proof of the talents of black people.

Thomas Jefferson exchanged letters with Banneker in 1791, nine years before becoming the president of the United States. ▼

kindness and benevolence toward them; and thus shall you need neither the direction of myself or other
in what manner to proceed herein.

And now, Sir, altho my Sympathy and affection for my brethren hath caused my enlargement
thus far, I ardently hope that your candour and generosity will plead with you in my behalf, when I m
known to you, that it was not originally my design; but that having taken up my pen in order to direct
you as a present, a copy of an Almanack which I have calculated for the Succeeding year, I was unex-
pectedly and unavoidably led thereto.

This calculation, Sir, is the production of my arduous Study in this my advanced Stage of life;
having long had unbounded desires to become acquainted with the Secrets of nature, I have had to gratify
curiosity herein thro my own assiduous application to Astronomical Study, in which I need not to reco
to you the many difficulties and disadvantages which I have had to encounter.

And altho I had almost declined to make my calculation for the ensuing year, in consequence of th
time which I had allotted therefor being taking up at the Federal Territory by the request of Mr. Andr
Elliott, yet finding myself under Several engagements to printers of this state to whom I had commun-
ted my design, on my return to my place of residence, I industriously applyd
have accomplished with correctness and accuracy, a copy of which I have taken the liberty to direct to
and which I humbly request you will favourably receive and altho you may have the opportunity of perusing
after its publication, yet I chose to send it to you in manuscript previous thereto, that thereby you might
not only have an earlier inspection, but that you might also view it in my own hand writing.

And now Sir, I shall conclude
and Subscribe my Self with the most profound respect
your most Obedient humble Servant

NB any communication to me
may be had by a direction to
Mr Elias Elliott merchant
in Baltimore Town

Benjamin Banneker

▲ In his letter to Thomas
Jefferson, Banneker called
for an end to slavery.

Later Years

Banneker published six almanacs from 1792 to 1797. The first ones sold many copies. Banneker made enough money from the almanacs to live comfortably, but they did not make him rich.

Growing Older

During the last few years of his life, Banneker stopped farming. He still grew a garden and continued studying astronomy. He began to experience the aches and pains of old age. It became hard for him to travel by horseback to town, but he still took daily walks around his farm. He never stopped reading books and studying the stars.

YEAR of our LORD 1795;
Being the Third after Leap-Year.

BANNAKER.

PHILADELPHIA:

Printed for WILLIAM GIBBONS, Cherry Street

Banneker's portrait appeared on the title page of his 1795 almanac.

On October 9, 1806, Banneker took his usual walk. He began to feel ill and went home. He lay down, and a short time later he died. He was one month away from his 75th birthday.

▲ In 1980, the U.S. Postal Service created a stamp to honor Banneker.

During the funeral two days later, Banneker's house burned to the ground. The Ellicotts saved some of Banneker's personal items, including his journal and his wooden clock. Everything else was destroyed. Over the years, his journal made its way to the Maryland Historical Society. But the clock has disappeared.

Banneker is one of the most respected early African American scientists. He proved that a person's intelligence is not determined by the color of one's skin.

Fast Facts

Name: Benjamin Banneker

Birth: November 9, 1731

Death: October 9, 1806

Home: Baltimore County, Maryland

Parents: Mary and Robert Bannaky

Siblings: three sisters

Education: Elementary school, self-educated

Achievements:

   Built a working clock using a pocket watch as a model

   Taught himself mathematics and astronomy

   Assisted in the surveying of Washington, D.C.

   Published several popular almanacs

Time Line

Life Events of Benjamin Banneker

Benjamin Banneker is born a free black person.

Banneker becomes owner of the family farm after the death of his father.

Banneker builds a wooden clock.

1731   **1753**   **1759**

Events in U.S. History

1732   **1754–1763**   **1775**

George Washington, future U.S. president, is born.

France and Great Britain fight the French and Indian War; the fighting takes place in North America.

Great Britain and the American colonies begin fighting in the Revolutionary War.

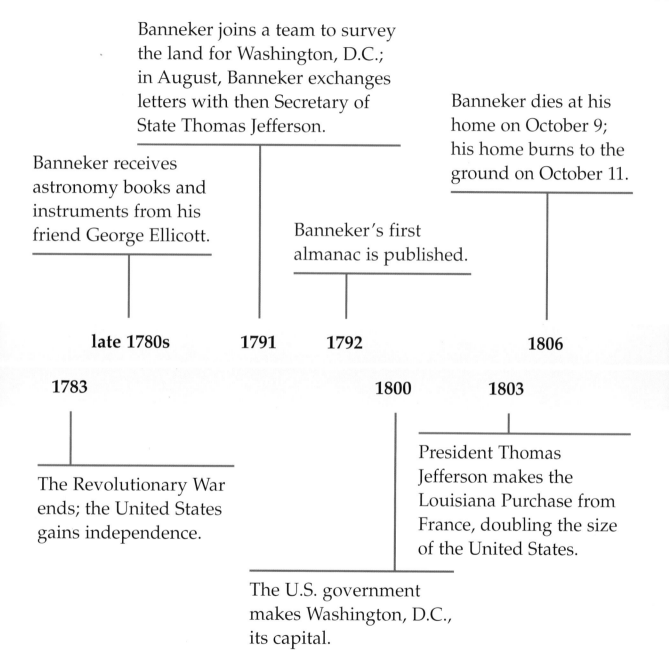

Banneker joins a team to survey the land for Washington, D.C.; in August, Banneker exchanges letters with then Secretary of State Thomas Jefferson.

Banneker dies at his home on October 9; his home burns to the ground on October 11.

Banneker receives astronomy books and instruments from his friend George Ellicott.

Banneker's first almanac is published.

late 1780s   **1791**   **1792**   **1806**

1783   **1800**   **1803**

The Revolutionary War ends; the United States gains independence.

President Thomas Jefferson makes the Louisiana Purchase from France, doubling the size of the United States.

The U.S. government makes Washington, D.C., its capital.

Glossary

almanac (AWL-muh-nak)—a book published once a year with facts, statistics, and predictions about a large variety of subjects, such as farming and weather

astronomy (uh-STRON-uh-mee)—the study of stars, planets, and space

observation (ob-zur-VAY-shun)—something you have noticed by watching carefully

prediction (pri-DIK-shuhn)—a statement of what somebody thinks will happen in the future

Quaker (KWAY-kur)—a member of the Society of Friends, a Christian group founded in 1650 that prefers simple religious services and opposes war

survey (SUR-vay)—to measure an area in order to make a map or plan

Internet Sites

FactHound offers a safe, fun way to find Internet sites related to this book. All of the sites on FactHound have been researched by our staff.

Here's how:

1. Visit *www.facthound.com*
2. Type in this special code **0736854320** for age-appropriate sites. Or enter a search word related to this book for a more general search.
3. Click on the **Fetch It** button.

FactHound will fetch the best sites for you!

Read More

Blue, Rose, and Corinne J. Naden. *Benjamin Banneker: Mathematician and Stargazer.* A Gateway Biography. Brookfield, Conn.: Millbrook Press, 2001.

Burke, Rick. *Benjamin Banneker.* American Lives. Chicago: Heinemann Library, 2003.

Wadsworth, Ginger. *Benjamin Banneker: Pioneering Scientist.* On My Own Biography. Minneapolis: Carolrhoda Books, 2003.

Index